The Language of Alcohol

A non-12 step program for Recovery and Relapse Prevention

BY

Phillip Wister MFT

The Empire Publishers publishing
12808 West Airport Blvd Suite 270M Sugar Land, TX 77478

https://empirepublishers.co/about-us

Our books may be purchased in bulk for promotional, educational, or business use.
Please contact The Empire Publishers at +(844) 636-4576, or by email at support@theempirepublishers.com

First Edition 2025

Dedication

This book is dedicated to my youngest son, Cleve Wister.

Our lives have paralleled in many of the formative experiences we have shared. Cleve has faced the challenge of addiction for many years, enduring periods of both struggle and sobriety. As of this writing, he has been sobered for two years. I am incredibly proud of the man he has become and the strength he has demonstrated in his journey to reach this point. His resilience and determination continue to inspire me.

Table of Contents

Foreword

I have had a long journey as a therapist. I have learned many things about the Human condition which have served me well in serving others who have come into my private practice. I cannot take full credit for the insights I lay down here because like most well-seasoned professionals, I stand on the shoulders of the giants from whose wisdom I was to benefit.

I have to pay homage first and foremost to my Stepfather. When I was 6, my Mother believed I needed a father and found an Irish alcoholic to make into that image. This was my alcoholic. My family, genetically, came from generations of teetotalers. No one drank and they did not have a dysfunctional set of family rules centered on alcohol. They had their own set of dysfunctional rules that proved adequate to sabotage their relationships and family structures. What I mean by `my alcoholic` is, this was the person brought into our family culture that introduced me to the culture and therefore the rules of the alcoholic family structure and function. This was the beginning of my journey to being a therapist. I will explain this later.

I owe a great deal of my self-esteem to Max Rose JD. My Uncle Max was a close working friend of my stepfather's, a drinking buddy, and the first person to really acknowledge my intelligence. He helped guide me through the pitfalls of my dysfunctional family in long afternoon discussions. This was really the first outside insight that something was dysfunctional with my upbringing. I always felt I let him down when it came to his own son. I think he saw my intelligence and raw empathetic ability and underestimated how emotionally immature I was and not yet evolved enough to deal with mentoring another human, his son Marshall.

I believe that Father Tim Fallon SJ saved my life. I got to my freshman year at Santa Clara University above my head and drowned emotionally. Father Fallon was the Dean of the Philosophy dept at Santa Clara. I have no idea how it worked out that he spent so many of his office hours doing what amounted to counseling with me. He walked me through many an existential crisis. I can really say that I contemplated taking my own life many times during freshman year. Father Fallon was the anchor, I believe, that kept me here. He liked orchids. He had his own space in the greenhouse behind the observatory on campus. I remember the calm I felt helping him water and care for his orchids. I still garden to this day for my mental health.

I must pay homage to one of the giants who guided me on my professional path. Cary Cochran MFT was an incredible Therapist and Teacher. He was my first supervisor and set me up with an outlook and orientation to this profession that has served me well in working with people from all backgrounds and human stripes. Cary told me that Therapists are born, then get training in school. He said that if you aren't born with the essential empathetic soul, you get training and become a technician. Technicians can do a write-up of an individual but not really understand or capture the emotional depth that human represents on the other side of the desk. Cary imparted a few pearls of wisdom I still follow to this day. He told me "Never outdress your clients".

This is intimidating to them. I have followed this strictly. He worked with the most difficult personality-disordered people. He did it well. This generated the second pearl of wisdom I received from him; "it's the relationship, stupid!" People will do well on their journey with you if they feel connected, comfortable, and safe. Thank you, Cary. This wisdom has its backing in research by Scott D. Miller et al, in the following: The Outcome of Psychotherapy: Yesterday, Today, and Tomorrow Scott D. Miller, Mark A. Hubble, Daryl L. Chow, and Jason A. Seidel. International Center for Clinical Excellence.

The last thank you I pay to Amanda Villaveces MFT. She was an Intern of mine whose skills far outpace my own. She did a little pushing to get me to put this into writing. She is a great Therapist that runs a clinic now back in Kentucky. You would do well to see her if you are in the Louisville area.

The Rules

1. We tell lies (either bald-faced lies or lies of omission).
2. We keep secrets.
3. We have to look good.
4. We avoid confrontation.
5. We find no resolution.
6. We are not emotionally honest.
7. We deny anything and everything.
8. We ignore the elephant in the room.
9. We are blind to the obvious.
10. We have no boundaries.
11. We have limited coping skills.
12. "YOU" is the main pronoun.
13. We have an External Locus of Control.
14. We make excuses for ourselves and others.
15. We live by "All or Nothing", there is no middle ground.
16. Shame, Blame, and Guilt are operational definitions.
17. We need a scapegoat (or identified patient).
18. We don't take responsibility.
19. We have silent expectations.

Introduction: The Language

I must start out with a guiding idea that governs my approach to therapy. Publius Terentius Afer was a Roman playwright who penned the idea; "Homo sum, Humani nil a me alienum puto."

I am Human; therefore I consider nothing human alien to me.

I introduce the Language of Alcohol to clients organically. I tell them the story of how I learned it. There are many similarities in how we learn these things growing up and I feel clients relate to this as a shared experience much better.

I grew up on one of those baby boomer blocks. There were always a million kids out in the street playing. We were the blossom of the boomer generation. Our dads were all WWII combat veterans up and down the block. They had seen and done some terrible things during the War. They were all now back safe and sound building the country. By the mid 50's they were secure in their positions and earned the right to sit on the stoop and drink themselves silly. They were just cooling down after work after all.

There were two types of dads in this scenario. The first Dad had an ice chest out sitting next to him with beers plunked down in the ice nice and neat. He was just cooling down after work. It was his time to chill and watch the kids play in front. Provide and protect, are the two main roles of the man in our culture. This sitting usually consisted of a six-pack or two of tallboys or many a thirsty swig from a bottle hidden strategically outside, depending on the recipients' built-up tolerance.

The second type of Dad hid his alcohol outside somewhere so he could drink 'undetected'. This was my stepfather. He was a rather short Irish man. When I turned 12, I was taller. He had a step ladder in the abbreviated garage we had. He would pull out his step ladder and climb it in front of the house and retrieve his bottle of whiskey from the gutter eve of the house. This was his strategic hiding place.

Of course, as kids playing in the street we could see all these little scenes play out every day. We saw our Dads come home after work and drink themselves silly on the stoop, every day. Our Dads were oblivious to our careful observation (rule no. 9). Soon it was getting toward dinner which our moms were dutifully preparing. They would call us in for dinner. Our Dads would give us the whistle, each family had their own distinct whistle, and we would follow them into dinner.

A very similar discussion would ignite the evening as our dads would stumble in the door. The first Dad, with the beers in the ice chest, open about cooling down after work, would be on the receiving end of the following dialogue;

Mom, "You are drunk!"

Dad, "No I am not."

The child learns "No" means "Yes".

This precursor set the tone for dinner and the rest of the evening. The discussion went back and forth with "You" being the main pronoun (rule no. 12) in use hurled across the table as the volume increased. As the kid in the situation, you were initially invisible as the focus was on the animosities and resentments that each parent had built up over time for each other. After all, it is hard to be emotionally present for your spouse if you were inebriated every night. You learned to eat really fast at that table because you did not want to be made part of the discussion for any infraction in the rules or abridgment of the system you might have inadvertently committed that day.

You went to your room and found something to take your mind off the noise, yelling, and banging on counters and walls that were occurring. You might get your homework done under duress, but not your best work. Report card comments always included a comment that you were capable of more but were not showing it. Sleep was always hard to come by especially if the arguing went on late into the night. It was always emotionally exhausting.

You would drag yourself out of bed to get to school in the morning and have black circles under your eyes. Inevitably, you would get the question from the teacher;

Teacher, "Johnny, is everything ok at home?"

Johnny, "Yup, everything is just fine."

You knew that if a call, any call came home questioning the perfect-looking family(rule no. 3), you were going to get it. What "it" was and the degree to "it" being perpetrated on you depended on a few factors. If Dad heard about "it" just as he walked in the door, you might get lucky, because Dad was going to sit and cool down after work and might get drunk enough to forget the issue. Alcohol was a priority after all. If it was brought up at the table, you were doomed. Suddenly, you became the focus of the issues in the house(rule no. 17) and were not going to get away from that table no matter how fast you ate.

The dialogue was only slightly different at the house where Dad hid his Alcohol(my stepfather).

Mom, "You have been drinking!"

Dad, "No I haven't."

The child learns the same lesson, "No" means "Yes".

And the scenario plays out generally in the same form with the same results as in the first scenario.

This is how you learn the Language of Alcohol. There is no harm and no foul in this. We learn this language honestly. Our parents don't wake up one day and say they are going to teach us a screwed-up language that is dysfunctional and will follow us into the future to screw up our relationships and families. No, they teach us what they know and what they grew up with. They are doing their best.

I only started to give it the label, The Language of Alcohol, because this is the lens that I learned it through. It can be learned in many ways and through many different mediums, but the rules and the language stay pretty much the same. The learning process is the same. We all do addiction the same way, whatever the external stimulus/substance (cocaine, alcohol, internet, porn, video games, gambling, meth, PCP, Marijuana, work, hoarding, food, weight lifting, running, chaos, etc). I tell clients, It is not the Alcohol that makes you the Alcoholic, it's the language and behavior that is exhibited. You can just replace the words Alcohol and Alcoholic with any of the above identified potential addictions and you will come out with the same behaviors and language in the process. These are habitual behaviors and speech patterns that have been learned and practiced over time, since birth in many cases. These are the fundamentals of addiction. These are the behaviors and language that are familiar, comfortable, and therefore feel safe to us. This is one reason addiction is so hard to break. People focus on the substance/stimulus and not the way they go about the addiction. Many people don't get that addiction is a learned behavior in a cohesive family system. There is genetics involved in this but as in my particular case, the language and behavioral learning process sometimes proves stronger than any. Genetic predisposition.

An example I like to borrow from the AA folks to illustrate this idea is that of the "Dry Drunk". This is a person that is an alcoholic, they have no alcohol in them, but they still act like an asshole. They still act out the part of the addiction, but they are now without the external stimulus/substance.

Lying

1. *We tell lies (either bald-faced lies or through silence or omission).*

Men and women lie differently according to their different vernaculars. We speak completely different languages between us, it is a wonder that we ever get together to cohabitate let alone procreate. Women are raised with their emotions. By the time they are 12 years old, they can exhibit on their face 1000 different emotions in a convincing manner that makes the observer believe they are actually experiencing that emotion. Women are good at this. They are more in touch with their feelings and expression of these. This is why they can look you in the eye and lie to you without any skip in the conversation. They can bald-faced lie and move on as if nothing happened.

We can speculate that this alternative vernacular or system of language is a product of our culture. Women in our culture for thousands of years are used to being second fiddle to men. I lay this cultural issue at the doorstep of Religion. I believe all the children of Abraham diminish the value of women in our culture, the Jews, the Christians, and the Muslims. This has placed misogyny as a cultural norm. In response to this cultural barrier, women developed ways to gain power on the sly. Language, the way they speak, and how they manifest emotions, form a perfect vehicle for this process.

For Women, this could come in the form of apparent subordination of needs.

Woman, "Oh you really don't need to get me roses for my birthday."

Man, "OK honey."

This is obviously not the end of the conversation. There is an implicit message and expectation (rule no. 19) here that men don't understand because they tend to be concrete in their communication process. Men find themselves in this double bind situation and find themselves on the short end of the power equation of this interaction.

Men will tell lies of omission primarily. We were never good at lying. This goes back to the fact that our sisters could express emotions and we could not. We lived by playground rules that said you were not allowed to cry. Implied in this was also that we were not allowed to express ourselves emotionally. We got limited to the feelings of "pissed off" or "OK". Our Moms could always tell when we were lying, it was written all over our faces. We were told to take it outside if our emotion(s), 'pissed off' ran to high.

We think somehow we are noble creatures. We like to tell all the parts of a story that make us look good (rule no. 3).

Man, "I ran into some friends from High School at the bar last night"

Woman, "That's nice, who did you see?"

Man, "Oh, I saw some guys from the football team."

What he leaves out is that he also saw Suzy and they went out to his car and did a little hanky panky just like old times in High School. This would change the tone of the night so he leaves out the whole section of this part. It makes him look bad(rule no. 3).

In both of these scenarios, there are expectations embedded with the communication that lead to miscommunication and sabotage of trust in the relationship. First, Expectations sabotage relationships. Those are the little emotional needs in the back of our heads that don't get met (rule no. 19) and then turn into resentments and animosities that we hold on to.

The answer to this is to just be honest (rule no. 1 and no. 5). It is a very hard lifestyle to live with lies. You have to know whom you lied to, then know whom they know and talk to so you can try and be consistent with what you told them. It turns into mental gymnastics that some of us master better than others, but none of us get it 100%. I have clients that harbor these lies from their partners and experience tremendous anxiety doing so. When they finally reveal the truth to their partners they end up feeling a weight off their shoulders that they did not understand they were carrying. All this time they have tried to manage a future outcome that they can’t control but still try. When they finally give up this fallacy, they understand that the consequence was not as bad as the anxiety produced by holding onto the lie.

Secrets

2. We keep Secrets.

We love to keep secrets in our addicted families. It comes as second nature to us.

The first inclination, whenever there is information coming out, is to not say anything. This comes from two different learning processes in our upbringing.

The first thing that we learn growing up in an addicted household is that nothing is predictable. Not only are things not predictable but things may escalate to an explosion at any moment with little or no provocation. This is the idea that we are always walking on eggshells in this environment. This contributes to an increase in our background anxiety and our trepidation to discuss anything to do with the family. You don't know what topics are "safe" to talk about and which are Taboo. The problem here is that the parameters change at the whim of the Alcoholic/Addict. So what you knew not to talk about yesterday may have changed today. This is the emotional chaos of the system. This becomes embedded in our behavior and the anxiety comes back to us when we venture into the realm of information that is not generally known to others outside the family system. Our anxiety becomes the guard rails of what information we feel comfortable letting out and tends to shift from day to day increasing that anxiety.

We learn in this home to rationalize anything and everything. As we have been sensitized to not incur the wrath or anger of the system, we are also cognisant that we don't want to harm the feelings of anyone else. We become oversensitive to this idea, knowing what it feels like to have the explosion directed at us. So we keep certain topics and issues to ourselves. We caretake others' emotions in the system and take responsibility for others' feelings(rule no. 10). This is a job we obviously cannot do and end up being very frustrated* trying. The insidious nature of this learned behavior is that we end up translating this seemingly "positive" characteristic into our future relationships. Little did we know that what seemed positive and helpful to others would sabotage our future happiness having this learned characteristic as second nature.

It is the above two learning processes that stimulate the anxiety that stops us from talking even about insignificant things. We remain guarded about some subjects to the extent of keeping them secret(rule no. 2), even though their revelation would not amount to anything earth-shaking in our lives. We learn this honestly within this system. It manifests itself in those little interactions with your significant other later on where they look at you confused and ask,

"Why did you think you couldn't tell me that?"

Our significant others don't understand why we have a need to not reveal some things(rule no. 1) or to hold on to something insignificant(rule no. 2). They catch us in little white lies about having taken out the garbage or having cleaned the bathroom. These are small little lies that do not matter in the big picture of things or even in the small picture. They are just second nature and come out. We are at a loss to explain

it.

One explanation I offer here is an upbringing issue. In the Alcoholic/Addict family system we are primed to be wary of the next blowup. We are vigilant of this potential at all times. We are walking on eggshells all the time. We are always behaving with the idea that we can control for this outcome, and thwart it before it rears its ugly head.

We cant and never were able to stop this from happening no matter how hard we tried.

How this programed us becomes apparent in our communication in later relationships. We still maintain that learned behavior of controlling information(rule no. 1, rule no. 2, and rule no. 6). We are not so much lying as we are trying to control and limit the information that we let out, because we are expecting a blowup and still have no idea what will be the trigger. Even little things led to blowups in our upbringing, so it is little things that we withhold or lie about that we get caught with and have no understanding why on either side of that communication.

Looking Good

3. We have to look good.

In Addicted Families, we must present to the outside world an image of perfection. We have to look like the all-American family. Not only do we need to look the part, but we also must appear so in other ways. There is a mentality of circled wagons in the family structure that everyone knows(rule no. 8) and in their own way plays a part in protecting knowledge of "Who we really are" from the outside world.

Every member of the family plays a role in this. Sometimes members of this family go out of their way to overachieve because the other insidious message we get in this family system is; it is never good enough.

Johnny is an outstanding baseball player. He goes to the diamond and plays every day. Pick-up games with his friends are his escape from the oppression of the house. He doesn't define it this way because he hasn't achieved insight into the situation yet. He just knows he is good at something for which he receives unencumbered praise from the outside world. This is an important learning process and an emotional boost because the praise he has been used to comes with strings attached and caveats. The parental/family attention he has gotten thus far is; from parents who rarely come to games or if they come they make some sort of scene which is a violation of the rules (rule no. 3). Later there always seems to be a critique of some kind for his performance and never just gets unvarnished praise.

Johnny has a sister, Jill. Jill doesn't have the physical prowess of her brother or at least has not been given the forum to exert such abilities. Jill also faces the background cultural misogyny that many women face growing up, that her brother(s) is more important to the family than she is. She finds a role in her family with her need to achieve (something, anything) and obtain that elusive praise/attention which she craves from emotionally distant or not-present parents or even ignoring parents, specifically, her father, and it never comes. She finds those things in the house to do that need to be done but that the main relationship in the house, namely the parents, are not taking care of. These are the things that are above Jill's emotional pay grade but she sees they need to be done.

So Jill takes on these adult tasks. She works hard at things she knows need to be done. She has seen them being done before, but she is still not sure how to do them or if she is doing a good job. She just knows that they are not getting done or being done consistently anymore. She has stepped up and gotten these adult tasks done.

The other insidious way Jill may find to get the attention she needs is negative. She may learn to act out, be rebellious, seek attention from males in her peer group against her parent's wishes, and work below her ability in school. She may go as far as cutting. All these are designed to get recognition in her family. Negative attention becomes better than no attention.

This is how we build terrible self-esteem in our children. Jill, while doing these tasks that she has stepped up to do, never gets any full sense of internal accomplishment. She is focused on the task and simultaneously is aware that at any moment someone may yell at her for not doing it right. She never gets to stuff this into her self-esteem bank. Likewise, her brother Johnny is a great baseball player. Without the unencumbered praise or the critique after the fact(Read; it wasn't perfect), specifically from his parents, he is left thinking that he is doing 'OK', but never is fully able to feel the accomplishment of his achievements.

This can turn into a lifelong habitual way of accomplishment. It gets learned as a way of doing things and we never seem to build solid self-esteem from the accomplishments we have achieved. We find ways to self-deprecate or point out better ways it could have been done. We are not quite able to accept the thank yous and kudos for what we have done. We are embarrassed to be called out for doing something well. We have a hard time accepting awards instead of thinking or voicing that we were only doing our job. This learning process becomes the basis of 'Imposter

Syndrome'. This syndrome is well-documented in the Mental Health world.

No Confrontation

4. No confrontation.

This rule of the Alcoholic family system stems in part from the unpredictable nature of the system. Everyone is always walking on eggshells. No one knows when the next blow-up or tirade is going to take place and who is going to be the recipient of the anger. This builds into us an anxiety that acts like behavioral guard rails. We modify or gauge our behavior and language based on what we think the system will tolerate at the moment. We are aware that this parameter may have changed overnight. We definitely don't want to draw attention to ourselves in this system. We know that we would then become the focal point of whatever reaction is going to happen, usually angry and negative. (There are instances where this may be sought out by one of the members of the system as in rule no. 3) We ingrain this aversion to confronting issues through this negative feedback loop and carry it forward into our future relationships.

Another contributing factor to this aversion to confrontation is rule no. 18, No

Responsibility. This is a recurring theme in the Addicted family. It forms the basis of a lot of the dysfunction that takes place. Because the main relationship in the family, Mom and Dad, are not taking responsibility for the emotions, responsibilities, or dysfunctions of the system, it leaves a power vacuum or responsibility gap. This sense of emotional absence in the family is a reason we start to see roles emerge from this system. The Fixer, the Goat or

Identified Patient, the Rebel, the co-dependent or enabler, and the lost child, are all roles that spring up around the main role, the Alcoholic/Addict. These roles are known by different names depending on the author. The above are my working labels.

The roles that develop are just different members of the system trying to cope with the dysfunction without taking it on or confronting it. There are a number of factors in how these roles shake out. Sibling position plays a factor where the oldest sometimes becomes the Identified Patient or the Fixer in order to draw abuse away from their younger siblings. They take on emotional responsibility (Rule no. 18) in the system that is above their emotional pay grade. The younger children in the system tend to get lost and never really get the attention they need from the primary relationship but never get their share of abuse from the system. The second child many times becomes the Rebel. They have a tendency to be more aggressive socially in any family but in an addicted family, they tend to Rebel. They know or have a sense that things are dysfunctional and rail against what they see as wrong to themselves or to their siblings. They tend to leave or get kicked out of the system because of their disruptive nature to the status quo. The status quo being the Alcoholic/Addict is in charge of the chaos generation in the system and cannot tolerate a rival to their power, the Rebel, in the system. Let me emphasize, the Rebel is not confronting the system, they are arguing against the system, a different process that has no capacity to bring resolution to the system.

At this point, defining the terms Confrontation vs Arguing is important. To confront someone, you must define how you feel and your needs in the interaction. You are demonstrating Emotional Sovereignty. This is a foreign concept in the Addicted family system. The roles that develop and the interactions that play out are all interdependent. There are no boundaries set between members of the system. Therefore, they don't have a good definition of themselves independent of the system This process serves the need of keeping the status quo in the system. They are not stand-alone roles. Whereas, the person who stands up for what they think, need, and want, are standing outside the system. They are Emotionally Sovereign. They are setting boundaries that the system is not used to and therefore disruptive to the system.

The language that is employed is far different and not tolerated by the system. A confrontation sounds like this;

"I really don't like to be put down."

"I don't think that comment was constructive."

"I need to be treated with respect."

These are all confrontational statements. They are clearly conveying the speakers wants needs and emotions. The speaker is standing on their Emotional Sovereignty. They are demonstrating their independence from the system and therefore they are a danger to the integrity of the system. They threaten the status quo.

"Why do you have to talk to me like that?"

"You are being very negative."

"You are not very respectful."

These are all examples of argumentative statements. They seem like they are confronting but they primarily are accusing the other party. They follow the rules of the system (Rule no. 12). They call "You" the main pronoun the accusative case in English for good reason. It is also a good demonstration of how we deal with responsibility (Rule no. 18) in addicted families like it's a verbal hot potato. No one wants to hold on to it, least of all the Alcoholic/Addict.

No Resolution

5. No Resolution.

Having issues in an addicted family keeps the system on edge at all times. There never is a shortage of issues or problems only an impediment to resolving them. It helps perpetuate the unpredictability of the system and therefore spreads the eggshells evenly for the various members of the system. We never finish arguments so that means there is always something left undone. This neglect leaves things open to criticism and the perpetuation of issues and potential arguments and future blowups.

A perfect example of this is in my story I tell clients how they learned this language. Imagine being the kid at that table where the argument is whether or not your father figure is drunk or has been drinking. You, of course, know the truth of this, ultimately holding onto the secret (rule no. 2). You eat fast to extricate yourself from the situation before being sucked into and becoming a part of the argument. You go to your room but the chaos does not end and is quite audible from where ever to you retreat. It does end at a certain point which may be after you have fallen asleep through exhaustion or desensitization to the process. Miraculously, in the morning, everyone is going about their defined roles, work, housework, or going to school, without a word or an acknowledgment as to what took place the night before. This is how we never get to learn the tedious skill of staying with an arguement/disagreement till a resolution is reached (rule no. 5).

We end up going to school with less than adequate sleep, not really sure what is going to take place when we get home. We spend little time at breakfast because meals have been learned as traps for us so we eat fast, not good for digestion. These are only a few of the distracting factors we must navigate through in our school day. We have to make sure that there is no call home for any reason. The teacher sees your distress and asks if everything is all right. You, cognizant of the rules (rule no. 3), don't want part of your day to garner a phone home and reflect poorly on the family.

“Yup everything is great.”

You know as a member of the system you must maintain secrecy (rule no. 2). This is reinforced by the knowledge that you suddenly will be the issue of the day if there is a call home from school. Even the most benign call of, ‘Is Johnny all right?’, ‘Is Johnny getting enough sleep?’. Your teacher meant well. She had your best interests in mind but did not understand the subtle consequences of this concerned act. The interrogation that took place at the dinner table was unbearable. You had no way out and knew that this was going to be the issue of the night and you were then the problem de jour. So you make up some story as to why you did not get any sleep last night(rule no. 1, male form) and the Teacher may or not buy it.

Self-blame (rule no. 16) is a mighty tool in the system that the members all seem to adhere to but which does not really exist unless they all play. The random intermittent blowup is the motivation for this belief and therefore the catalyst that keeps the system going. In the behavioral sciences, the strongest reinforcement technique is an intermittent reinforcement schedule. In these much-replicated experiments, 'rats are trained fastest in this manner and the learning is then very hard to undo.' *

It is no wonder so many kids are misdiagnosed in school with ADD or ADHD. This has been a problem in schools for some time and it makes one wonder if addicted homes are an essential cause of this quiet epidemic.

*Intermittent reinforcement is programmed on a schedule of reinforcement, with responses being reinforced on random intervals of time (e.g., time since the last reinforcement) or number of reinforcements (e.g., every nth response is reinforced). Basic schedules of reinforcement generate extremely strong reinforced patterns of behavior, and in my example for this treatise creates a cohesive system of allegiance to a dysfunctional system (Ferster & Skinner, 1957).

No Emotional Honesty (to ourselves or others)

6. No Emotional Honesty

This type of dishonesty is quite different from rule no. 1(Lying). We are trying to mask our feelings or try to caretake others' emotions rather than acknowledge them and understand their origin. We also are blind to our own emotions that come out in the addicted family system (rule no. 9). The role of the codependent in this system is a good example to examine here. This is the mom (using stereotypical roles) that goes along with the Alcoholic/Addict husband, that helps the alcoholic continue his life course of addiction(s). Her job is caretaking his emotions, making sure he can function to the level he needs to provide for the family and get to his job, to be that "functional" Alcoholic/Addict.

Her emotions rise up periodically in a blowup which she considers confrontation (rule no. 4) but is really arguing and amounts to no resolution (rule no. 5). She sets no boundaries around these behaviors (rule no. 10) and therefore there are never solid consequences for the behaviors other than the random blow up, which is randomly endemic to the system anyway. There is no real reason for a change to happen in this system. Without consequences, boundaries mean nothing.

The impetus to leave the situation is almost always verbalized in the heat of battle but rarely acted on for very insidious reasons. First, I go back to the inculturation of little girls in our society. They are raised to be emotional but also to caretake others' emotions, especially their emotionally inept Male counterparts. They are good at emotions so they end up dealing with what they know best, caretaking other's emotions. They buy into the notion that they are the Peace Maker, a powerful role if that is actually the end result. As it plays out, this role is illusionary and the power position strived for never reaches any form of satisfaction. Arguments are only smoothed over till the next random blowup and they end up perpetuating no resolution (rule no. 5). They feel they are helping people in the system to get along. In the final analysis, the behavior ends up as one of the perpetuating factors in the dysfunctional system.

Second, women are second-class citizens in Western culture at the very least. As I stated before all the children of Abraham promote misogyny in their culture and put down their women, the Jews, the Christians, and the Muslims. Women, through their emotional prowess, are able to garner power in the addicted family system (and beyond) by their caretaking of others' emotions. They see themselves as holding the family together. They see themselves as the central figure of the family, which also looks like a powerful role. It gives a false sense of power within the dysfunctional system. So they stay, clinging to yet another illusion of social power.

In the practice of this rule "One's wants, needs, and desires end up being suppressed because they are not being talked about out loud. This of course works itself out along gender lines".* We have a tendency because of our upbringing in this system to deny our own needs in our relationships and attempt to please or make happy our partners(rule no. 13). It only carries the illusion of working until that blow-up or argument comes that we don't understand but rears itself into our relationships anyway.

What we are not understanding is the stress of suppressing our needs. These don't go away, they just fester like a splinter that has been in your hand too long. It needs to come out. Our emotions need to be expressed. The longer we hold them in, the more likely they are to come out in ways that we are not controlling. We get irritable, make snarky comments, and end up starting arguments that seem to come from nowhere. * Acknowledgement to Alain de Botton The School of Life

Deny Anything and Everything

7. Denial

I have always been fond of the pun, "Denial, ain't just a river in Egypt". It's corny but conveys an essential message, we all find denial useful at times in our life. In addicted families, it is one of the mechanisms that keep the system in balance. It removes the needless interference of truth that always seems to creep into the addicted family system from the outside world. Truth is always a disruptive element to this closed system. Those things that we have been told are good for us or bad for us at some point get discovered as different when the reality of them is tested by any of the members of the system.

The first type of denial is one that we don't even realize. Here is an all too common story I hear in my practice. Mom and Dad have come in to see me about their children. They don't understand where they got these behaviors. Johnny is out drinking and carousing and beating up girls. Jill is out drinking and carousing and getting beaten up by boys. We came from horrible households. Our parents were horrible alcoholics. They were terrible parents. We hated our upbringing. So we resolved to never have alcohol in the house. We never drank. We always told our kids how bad it was for them. What did we do to deserve this kind of behavior from our children? We raised them better than that.

These parents don't even understand that they were the ones that raised their children. They were the ones their children looked up to for guidance. Children watch what we do and say and don't listen to what we tell them to do. They are great observers. This is how they learn. These parents learned all their lessons well from their Alcoholic Family systems. They passed all these lessons on to their children. They feel they left out the only issue that corrupted the system, Alcohol. They in fact don't understand that it isn't the alcohol that makes the alcoholic or corrupts the system, it is the Language and Behavior that they learned and was and integral part of their parenting. In fact, they are in complete denial that it was their language and behavior on which the system of their family was built. This is not only following rule no. 7 but also typifies rule no. 9, Blindness to the Obvious. Who raised their children? What house were those children raised in?

The other kind of denial is quite blatant. No secret that when we struggle with addiction, it is easy to relapse. This just means we are following the rules still as I have been outlining. When the Alcoholic says, “It won't hurt to have just one beer”, or the Addict says, “There is just a small amount left I will quit after”. The cigarette smoker that says I won't buy another pack after this then is puffing off others' smokes or borrowing. This is the highest form of denial; ‘I am going to use to stop using it.’ I deny my part in the process. I deny that the substance or stimulus is a problem at that moment. The Addict has circled back to just being an addict in verbal backflips of rationalization. Some call this relapse. I consider this situation that the Alcoholic/Addict never left the process of addiction, they just were not using their substance/stimulus for a specific time, a dry drunk as the AA folks like to label it.

It is clear that through either of these avenues, denial (rule no. 7) has a dramatic effect on the family system. It is subtle but effective in reinforcing the language and behaviors of addiction through generational learning. Clients, when confronted with this realization, will sometimes get a negative attitude, either they feel blamed (once again, rule no. 16) for something that they feel they did not do, or they feel shame that they did this to their children (rule no. 16 again).

What I tell these befuddled parents and individuals is that there are no good guys and bad guys in this process. We teach our children what we know. We don't wake up one day and decide to teach them a language and model behaviors that will screw up their future relationships and make them less effective at navigating their world socially. No. We do our best. With what resources we have, how we grew up, what we have learned, how much stress we are under, and how much therapy we have done to overcome our discovered ineffective behaviors. I tell them always, 'don't beat yourself up, you did your best'.

Pet Elephant in the House

8. We ignore the Elephant in the room

This happens in many households. It is very common in how we dysfunction in western culture in our families. There are those specific topics that we all know as a group or a family, that are not to be spoken about.

In my family, there was a barrier when it came to talking about anyone's health or medical issues. This was strictly off-limits for no apparent reason. I was the only healthy person physically in my family. Dental appointments or Doctor appointments were not shared with other family members. There was always a rationalization; 'we don't want to alarm them', 'they have enough to worry about', or 'they don't really need to be burdened with that information'. This was very weird because I was in the best health of anyone, but there lies why this had to be a rule.

My mother's addiction early on became food. She was looking for comfort in that dopamine rush when you consume food, especially with high sugar content. She gained weight from her svelte days as a United States Marine to weighing over 500 lbs at her largest. I never knew when she had a Doctors appointment, nor did my step-father. It was this secretive (rule no. 2 and 8) venture that she carried out without anyone knowing. Weight more than anything was the issue that killed her in the end.

The other prime example of the elephant in my house was my stepfathers' health. He was, as I have stated, the Alcoholic/Addict in the house. It was the open secret that he had bad teeth and always suffered from stomach disorders.

It was Ileitis Terminalis, or it was Diverticulitis or any number of issues the Doctors would speculate on according to him. He was the source of information because my mother was never allowed to attend any of his appointments with him. He blamed his teeth deteriorating on the Military dental care during his service in World War II. He would say that his genes were bad, yet his older sister who lived in town had a better set of teeth still (rule no. 6). There were numerous excuses (rule no. 14) but they all added up to dodging the real issue, his use of Alcohol (rule no. 9, or no. 14 as stated). His consistent blood/ alcohol level is what leached calcium from his system to deteriorate the enamal from his teeth.

His stomach issues were obviously a function of his constant inebriation. His constant alcohol consumption caused an irritation of his colon which is what Ileitis Terminalis is. These all fit into a pattern of behavior following the rules (rule no. 7, rule no. 8 which I am outlining here, and rule no. 9). He was of course the only source of what the Doctor told him which was an issue. He was careful to stay away from alcohol for a day or so before appointments to avoid the obvious call-out on the blood work he would be required to do. I am sure that his liver told the Doctor what really was going on. In his later years, my mother insisted on going to the appointments. The story was dramatically different then. He was being told you are going to die if you keep up drinking on this scale.

He did cut down from two six-packs of beer a day to a case of near beer, which still had alcohol in it(rule no. 3,6, and 9). He just had to drink twice as much to get his blood alcohol up to his therapeutic level. The hilarious part of this was that he had to get up every 10 minutes to go to the bathroom, ironically giving him more exercise than he normally would take, silver lining.

Blindness to the Obvious

9. We are blind to the obvious

This rule is that leap of faith we take when we make stuff up to fit our narrative (rule no. 3 plays a part in this). We have a tendency to believe our own made-up narrative as to how things are going in our lives and how they were in our history. There is some research in Memory in the Neuroscience field that supports this idea that we fill in our memories where they are not quite complete and these tend to be beneficial to our narrative histories.

I gave the example narrative of the parents that come in and are concerned about their kids and how they never had alcohol in the house. Alcohol was the focus of their idea of what was dysfunctional in their families of origin (rule no. 9). Of course, it was the Language and Behaviors manifested in those families to maintain the addict and the system of addiction in the family. The last thing the parents think is that somehow they are the ones responsible (rule no. 18) for these errant behaviors they see in their children. This is the essence of this dysfunction (rule no. 9). They are oblivious to their impact on the upbringing of their own children.

An incident in my past that solidified this point (rule no. 9) was demonstrated very succinctly by my Mother. She was at my house visiting her grandchildren. She was sitting at the table which because of her size, was the only place in the house where she could sit and then get back up to her walker (rules no. 3 and 8). I was talking on the phone to a friend of mine, Lance Ryen LCSW, who was and is an incredible Therapist in his own right. He at that point had 20 some years of sobriety through AA and his own perseverance. I was telling him about the idea I had about these rules I had figured out I had learned growing up with an Alcoholic/Addict, in an alcoholic family system. He confirmed to me some of the same ideas and experiences I had growing up. He was very helpful with the stories of his own journey through addiction and that family system.

As I was sharing some of my experiences of abuse and learning in my family of origin, my Mother at the table started crying. This confused me because I was by this point getting rather clear-eyed on my upbringing and honest about its effect on my general social abilities in my relationship with my wife, my parenting, my work relationships, and my outside social interactions. These all were affected by the Language and Behavior that I learned in this system growing up. I was coming to realize the extent to which it was sabotaging me in all these areas.

There was my mother sitting at the table crying. I asked her, not so politely, 'Why are you crying?' As this seemed to come out of the blue for me (rule no. 12).

She said, "I thought I protected you from all of that" (a prime example of rule no. 9).

I asked her, "What house do you think I grew up in?" (again rule no. 12).

She was completely oblivious to the idea that I would somehow learn something different other than what was demonstrated in front of me (rule no. 9) for literally years. She was blind to the abuse that took place in front of her.

My stepfather would 'teach me Boxing' at 9 years old. I was a big kid, but it was inappropriate and as I have come to realize, it was his way to beat the crap out of me for no apparent reason, since I rarely stepped out of line. I knew that the next explosion was right around the corner and I did not want to be the ignition.

This one incident solidified this idea (rule no. 9).

On further review of this interaction, I realized that I was following the rules (rule no. 9 and rule no. 12). She was the one that helped teach me these rules and I was oblivious at that moment to understand that I had descended back into that dysfunctional language and behavior pattern of my family system.

I need to point out here that these rules are easy to fall back into. We grew up with them. They are first nature to us. We have to be constantly vigilant that we are not backsliding or relapsing into the old way of doing things. We need to continue to break these rules until a more effective way of living becomes first nature. The rules are posted on my refrigerator to this day.

No Boundaries

10. We have no boundaries.

Therapists like to talk about Boundaries. This topic always sneaks its way into sessions overtly in that the Therapist harps on it, and some do. It also enters covertly when someone makes the realization in the session that they are being put down, dismissed, treated like an object, or otherwise micro-aggressed. These transgressions happen subtly. They follow a pattern of Language and Behavior that flies under the radar of almost all of us that grow up in this type of environment. We don't see the micro-aggressions until we SEE the micro-aggressions. When we make that realization it is like a wart suddenly appearing on our face that seemed to be there the whole time (rule no. 9).

Boundaries of course are not foreign to many other ways of dysfunctioning in family systems. Alcoholic/Addict families have no monopoly on boundary violations by their members. It does not manifest itself any differently either, other than having the added exacerbation of intermittent inebriation involvement and periodic explosive behavior to let off stress in the family system.

I have seen many examples of boundary violations in my 30 years of practice. I like the pet example to demonstrate this rule in an alcoholic family. Everyone likes a pet. Americans are obsessed with their pets. It fills out the all-American family look. It is integral to the all-American family (rule no. 3).

Dad, in this case playing the role of the Alcoholic, Impulsively wants to get a puppy. He says this in passing,

‘Wouldn't it be nice to have a dog?’, or ‘The kids would really like a dog’. Some minor discussion is had. Mom, playing the role of the codependent, brings up the added stress and responsibility this would entail. There is a back-and-forth discussion about the merits and then the conversation just fades away (rule no. 5). Then without further communication, a week or so later, Dad takes the excited kids to get a puppy (rule no. 13). There was no warning about this to other significant member of the family, Mom. There was no real discussion or further discussion about this, it is just one more random occurrence, courtesy of the Alcoholic/Addict, that happens in the family that is not a blowup, but will lead to a blowup. Not all the eggshells you walk on are crunchy. Later, the blowup comes when Mom brings it up; ‘There was no discussion about this’, ‘Who is going to take care of it?’, and a few other objections that more than likely lead to that explosive argument.

He has ready answers for this before or during the blowup; ‘The kids will take care of it we can teach them responsibility (rule no. 18).’ The Alcoholic, of course, will not take responsibility with most of their behaviors geared to this end. In this instance, the responsibility gets pushed on the Codependent, Mom to enforce care for the puppy and clean up the mess, etc. This is a total violation of Mom’s Emotional Sovereignty.

Where the boundary violations happen is subtly manifested through the non-decision discussion. None of the issues brought up regarding the responsibility of the puppy are taken seriously (rule no. 18). The kids are put upon to be the driving force (rule no. 14) behind getting the puppy (rule no. 1, 6, and 18 a hat trick). The kids are also taught a clear lesson, you make yourself happy by getting stuff(rule no. 13). The wife, in this scenario playing the role of the codependent, is now solely responsible for this puppy. It is going to need to be fed, walked, and otherwise cared for in perpetuity. She follows through with this added responsibility to her already overflowing plate for all the reasons above. She does not rock the boat other than to cause another blow-up by making an issue of it. It becomes one more thing to be brought up in the next inevitable argument that is going to take place. The Alcoholic/Addict comes back to this, of course, as "that was in the past", or "Can't you let that go". The Alcoholic/Addict, the dad in this scenario, is not and will not take responsibility (rule no. 18).

The codependent, mom in this scenario, is the receptacle of the responsibility and emotions of the Alcoholic and the family system. She is treated as an object, she is burdened with responsibility, and she is ganged up on with the kids being foils in the shame/blame game (rule no.

16) and becomes the scapegoat if the impulsive adventure fails (rule no. 17), which it inevitably does.

Limited Coping Skills

11. We have limited coping skills

Just about every behavior and every sentence uttered in the vocabulary of the Alcoholic/Addict have to do with the limited coping skills they acquired growing up and throughout their lives. They learned these skills, language, and behaviors honestly. Their Parent(s) were great role models for these. I would be notating rule no. 11 after every example and the point I make in this treatise because this is so pervasive in the development of the Language and Behavior of the Alcoholic/Addict and the family system that develops around them.

We naturally get comfortable and used to the flow of the family system that we grow up in. It is the only example of what we know to be a family. So when the main character in this family blows up randomly and yells at us for no apparent reason, we learn to walk on eggshells, lay low, not make waves, and conveniently disappear out of the house for as long as we feel it is safe. The coping skill here is to find something that looks good (rule no. 3) outside the house which takes us away from the chaos of home. We excel at sports, we spend the night at a friend's house, and we spend a lot of time in our room "doing homework".

Through this learning, we develop coping skills that don't necessarily work well in the real world but help us function and survive the dysfunctional system we are born into and learn through. In those now inevitable arguments that will crop up in our relationship(s), we shut down (rule no. 5). We go out for a drive. We dismiss the argument of our partner that makes the argument (rule no. 7). We spend a lot of time at work. Ultimately, we reach for the low-hanging fruit on the coping tree an external object or substance. We have a hard time and never really learned to deal with the emotions involved in relationships. Our role models were nearly devoid of legitimate emotional intimacy or honesty (rule no. 6).

We check out emotionally even though we remain present physically (rule no. 3). We have this erroneous idea that no one knows (rule no. 9). We think we are fulfilling our father role just by being there and don't realize that we are not (rule no. 9). Our emotional presence is required for the support of the family. Without our emotional presence, we become a fixture (rule no. 8). The kids talk about us behind our backs, "Gee, Dad was really baked tonight huh?." Our wives in this scenario are tired of not having us around emotionally but saying nothing to us as they make their own plans (rule no. 6).

I had a client come into my practice afraid that he was addicted to Marijuana. He had an incident where he was caught with his stash at the airport. He did a lot of traveling for his seemingly quite successful career with a large international company. He was scared and genuinely felt this for maybe the first time in his life (rule no. 6). He had smoked consistently since he was 14. He was home every night. Ate dinner with the family. Watched TV with his wife and kids coming in and out of the scene. He felt he had a perfect life, except for this one little incident at the airport. This was an excuse (rule no. 14) and a misdirection from the real issues confronting him for his need to smoke daily. He felt he was addicted and wanted to quit (rule no. 14). I applauded this motivation even though I knew it was off base for the real reasons he should be quitting.

After several sessions of cajoling him to try medication for his obvious Bipolar condition, he got on meds. He had this feeling that meds were bad and marijuana was natural and therefore good (rule no. 15). He discovered he no longer had a need to smoke. This isn't the only thing he discovered. Suddenly, when he was present emotionally he realized that his kids knew he was baked every night and would make jokes and have fun with how out of it he was. In discussions with his wife, which he could finally coherently have, he discovered that she was thinking of divorce.

At work, even though he had awards for his sales under his belt, his coworkers all knew that he was stoned most of the time and capable of so much more. They accepted this because he was somewhat productive. His production dramatically increased after getting on meds and dropping marijuana. He was the only one surprised at the office as his coworkers saw his potential, but just never said anything (rule no. 4).

To be noted here, addiction often is a mask for a Bipolar condition. It is the workaround that they find to help them cope with a metabolism that sabotages their effective abilities. In the good old days before modern pharmacology, alcohol was used as a mood moderator. I tell people with Bipolar conditions that they are in good company with Mozart, and Edgar Allen Poe, to name a few.

“YOU” as the main Pronoun

12. “YOU” is the main pronoun

The premise of my treatise is that the language that we speak leads to our addictions. It governs our relapses. It dysfunctions our relationships. It is the pervasive communication tool with the outside world that illuminates our basic learned upbringing flaws. We learned growing up that responsibility was a hot potato that every member of the family system tries to toss to another. No one wants to take responsibility (rule no. 18), as modeled by the Alcoholic/Addict, so we were always pointing the finger or tossing the responsibility to someone else in the system. This necessitates a focus on the language we use away from ourselves (accusative case in English) in this system to focus on others in the system (third person, or accusative case in English), or “you” (rule no. 12).

When we grow up in this Alcoholic/Addict environment we learn the social end of this communicative process. We use it as a survival skill in a chaotic environment. It then is practiced through our upbringing where it becomes the norm, what we know, and therefore becomes comfortable. Then we end up putting it into practice when there is no chaos, it does not work. It comes off as awkward, or ineffective. As with all skill sets that have worked for us in the past, we tend to double down and force this skill. It still doesn't work. Our problem is that we did not learn other skills of communication or coping (rule no 11) and we get stuck in a loop of dysfunctional interaction. Our communication with anyone outside the system is skewed, and ineffective for the message we want to convey to those outside the system. The consequences of this are obvious, "I don't feel heard", or "They just don't understand me".

The use of "you" in the conversation is abrasive on a micro level (rule no. 12). We don't quite get why we feel put upon when we hear it but we do. It initiates a negative interaction that doesn't always end in an argument but starts out in that general direction. This likelihood doubles when we are attempting to give feedback.

"You put the dishes in the dishwasher that way and they didn't get clean." "You can't put the whites in with the colored clothes when you do the wash."

"Where did you learn to make a bed?"

These will all initiate a conversation as seemingly benign feedback into a negative spiral in which the interaction may not come to a congenial conclusion.

"The dishes will get cleaner when they are put in this way."

"If the whites and colored clothes are together, the whites will come out poorly."

"The bed looks better when it is made this way."

Or the communication can be more forceful or confronting in the following ways.

"I need the dishes put in the dishwasher this way."

"Please wash white and colored clothes separately."

"I need the bed made this way."

How we use language means a great deal as to how our message is communicated and received. We are not always heard when our language is ineffective or abrasive. Coming from the Alcoholic/Addict family system, we learn a language that is embedded with ineffectiveness and micro aggressiveness. It is what we know and how we learn to approach the world. Unfortunately, it is also a skillset that holds us back at times with this embedded ineffectiveness and sabotages us socially, at work, and in relationships.

External Locus of Control

13. We have an External Locus of Control

Of the rules, this is the one that people understand the least but get it, when explained. It is the most insidious and goes right to the heart of the Alcoholic/Addict family system. It is a cornerstone of how we learn to approach the world from this background. It dictates our orientation socially and to the world generally.

How I get people to understand this, I take them through Socratic dialogue.

"Did you graduate High School?"

Most of the time I get a "yes". Once in a while, I get embarrassed because they didn't and I have to backtrack on my accomplishment question.

If the client answered "yes", then I ask them, "Can I take it from you?"

This is the telltale answer as to their orientation to the world. If I have assumed correctly based on my experience, they will answer in the following ways.

"It is already done"

"It happened in the past"

These answers show that they first and fundamentally don't take responsibility (rule no. 18) for their accomplishment. It is a third-person point of view(rule no. 12). It is something that they have defined with the language as outside themselves. They don't own the accomplishment. They defined it as having an external origin or basis by the language and therefore, their general orientation to the world.

Someone Oriented to an Internal Locus of Control will inevitably give the following answer(s).

"I did it."

"I finished it."

"It's mine."

They own it. They accomplished it. They take the responsibility that accompanies this accomplishment and their language matches the reality. They learned to stuff it as one more accomplishment in their self-esteem bank.

In Addiction, we are utilizing an external object or idea to create a different feeling within us. I take this Cocaine, snort it, inject it, or otherwise put it in my body and I feel better. Usually, we are looking for the opposite of how we are feeling. So, I put this Alcohol in my body, I feel better. I put this Heroin in my body, I feel better. I put this Nicotine in my body, I feel better. I watch this Porn, I feel better. I pull this Slot Machine handle, I feel better, etc. As stated before, It is not the Alcohol that makes you the Alcoholic. It is not the Cocaine that makes you the addict. It is the Language and the Behaviors that make you the addict. The Rules are allpervasive. We grew up with them. We feel comfortable and safe in this communication process. It is, after all, the only way of doing things we know to this point. They led us into addiction because we were not addicts as children or even into adolescents. We stumbled into this way of doing things within the context of our upbringing which started with the language and behaviors we learned in our family system.

This way of orienting to the world inhabits everything we do. We learned it honestly from our parents. We could have been that kid whose parent took them to Toys R Us as a sidelight to going shopping because we did not want to go. Our Christmases were extravagant because giving, and especially receiving, was what the Holiday was about. We are driven as a culture in the United States to consume and feel good with the more we can consume. "Bigger is better". It all boils down to feeling good through some external object or means. In this, our culture reinforces this dysfunctional lifestyle and orientation to our reality coming from an Alcoholic/Addict family system. On a larger basis culturally, capitalism reinforces this through our society.

Excuses

14. We make excuses for ourselves and others

Excuses are a common human dodge of personal or group responsibility. It appears in many types of dysfunctional families whether or not there is an Alcoholic/Addict process happening. It should be no surprise that it shows up in the Alcoholic/Addict family system also. I cannot judge whether Excuses have any unique qualities in this system. I can only outline the ways that these reinforce this particular family system.

We already have learned that the Alcoholic/Addict process relies on an external locus of control (rule no. 13). So the first direction of our blame mechanism (rule no. 16) which is deeply entwined with the excuses we invent is, others. It is convenient to have brothers and sisters in this process, the more to blame the merrier.

"Jeremy said he would sweep the floor. It's his fault."

"Rachael used the car and didn't put gas in it. Why are you blaming me?"

"Why didn't Katie clean the bathroom last week when she was here?"

"It was too wet outside to rake leaves."

When it is my job or responsibility to sweep the floor, when I am using the car last, or when I am home and haven't cleaned up after myself, excuses become a mechanism to shift responsibility to something or someone external from ourselves(rule no. 13 and 18).

The example of getting the pet dog for the kids that I outlined earlier is a great example of setting up the whole mechanism of excuses. The discussion is briefly had that it would be nice to have a puppy. The kids would love it(rule no. 3). They would be in charge of feeding and taking care of it(rule no. 18) and with this statement, it is understood that the default caretaker is the codependent, the mom, in the example I outlined. It is an airtight little system that is set up for the Alcoholic/Addict to bail out when it fails, and because of the impulsiveness of the adventure, it mostly fails.

Another example would be from my childhood. We used to have to drive our garbage to the landfill when I was a kid. It was part of Sunday chores. We would gather everything from inside and outside the house and put it in the back of the truck to drive it out. Now the truck was a 1931 model A Ford pickup. I elaborate on this because this was one of the impulsive must haves that my stepfather made. It cost a great deal and set us back quite a bit. The household finances took a long time to recover from this purchase (rule no. 10, 13, and 18, a hat trick).

I was always in charge of the inside household refuse. I would collect everything from the laundry room garbage, under the sink in the kitchen, the bathrooms' garbage that needed to be emptied and take it out to the truck. My stepfather would be in charge of the garbage on the outside of the house. This could be grass clippings, leaves, and any leftovers from projects that he might be tinkering with outside the house.

This was a very convenient arrangement because my stepfather of course would hide his bottle outside in the gutter eve of the house (rule no. 8 and rule no. 9 on my mom's part). So he would have his stepladder pulled out of the garage and load something in the truck and then fetch his hidden bottle and take a drink. He would load more stuff in the truck and then take a drink. This went on till we had the truck loaded and then it would be time to drive out to the landfill. Here's what happened next.

We would check in with my mother at a distance, usually a call into the house that we were leaving. Then he would tell me that I was going to drive. He was way too inebriated to drive and had the good sense to know it. I was 12 years old. I was a big kid for my age. I could reach the pedals and see out the window. I was scared. The lie was he was going to teach me how to drive (rule no. 1). This was of course an elaborate excuse for him being too drunk to drive (rule no 14). This was apparent because he always said, "Don't tell your mother." (rule no. 2) So I would drive out to the landfill on Sundays. Thankfully in that era, there were no houses out there just roads and barren fields and very little traffic.

The most blatant excuses are the ones that include continuing the addiction. The cigarette smoker that is going to quit at the end of this pack or carton. The alcoholic whose plan is going to limit their intake to 2 drinks at a time. They may want to finish what is in their refrigerator or wine rack before they quit. The gambler that goes back to the ATM multiple times with the idea that they will win it back this time. The Foodie that goes for seconds or thirds and says to themselves that they will stay on the treadmill that much longer. These are all conspiratorial excuses (rule no. 14) we tell ourselves as addicts. They are those little rationalizations we utilize to stay comfortably ensconced in our addiction, no matter what the object of addiction is.

All or Nothing, there's no grey

15. We live by "All or Nothing", there is no middle ground

Many of us grew up hearing the phrase, "It's my way or the Highway." Another take-off of this was, "What I say goes." For the people behind these concise phrases, the world is black and white. There was no negotiation, resolution (rule no. 5), or grey area to discuss issues. It had to be a simple answer. In the Alcoholic/Addict family, this was a serious breaking point. It was one of the few coping mechanisms afforded the Alcoholic/Addict. Cut off any discussion that would complicate 'my world'.

This form of coping (rule no. 15) came to me in counseling people on how to deal with stress. One of the strategies I profess is to lessen what is on your plate. It's a common Therapy intervention. Clients will tend to take on all these things in their life at once and then they feel overwhelmed and don't know where to begin. I tell them things like 'make a list and only put 3 things on it'. The goal obviously is to find some success or accomplishment to spur you on to get more things done and feel better. Culturally and more importantly emotionally, we always feel better when we get things done.

The Alcoholic/Addict utilizes this strategy organically. They cut off all debate about any issue in single-phrase maxims.

"You don't like it, you can leave."

"It's my way or the highway."

“What I say goes.”

“I pay the bills here.”

I never realized till much later that this was a coping mechanism, one of the few (rule no. 11), that was employed to fend off a difficult conversation or narrow or end the discussion too complicated to process.

It came to me while thinking about and formulating the rules, that this was one of the ways the Alcoholic/Addict does to cope. Any kind of stress is a disaster and leads to a sure blow-up in the system. Stress added upsets the system and contributes to the next blow-up. By narrowing down the options for behaviors or discussion in the system, the stress goes down, the world is more predictable for the Alcoholic/Addict. There is less to process. It is the main reason we don't ‘step out of line’ as a member of the system. We instinctively understand the rules. We define it as walking on eggshells or not wanting to hurt someone's feelings. We know that anything outside the black or white, the more predictable, will throw stress into the system and cause the next blow-up for sure, and we will be the focus of the blow-up being the bringer. Growing up in this, we spend most of our energy avoiding this outcome. It is a brick wall that creates the space for a confrontation but we avoid this at all costs (rule no. 4). We are always on guard which creates physiological issues that will come up later in the form of panic attacks or ulcers.

There are a few problems that arise from this rule and this form of coping. It reinforces the rigidity of the system which in turn reinforces the need for a blowup. The rebel child in the system accommodates this need when they always stir up trouble when they see the emotional error inherent in this rigid system. They rebel and this calls into question the legitimacy of the system. The system collapses into chaos under external scrutiny or internal criticism.

Shame, Blame, and Guilt as operational explanations

16. Shame, Blame, and Guilt are operational definitions

Something I tell clients when I hear any of the shame blame guilt words or good and bad or sin. Cut these words out of the sentence just spoken and replace them with the word responsibility. I ask them to say it again in the new sentence. Then I ask them if they are responsible for whatever it was that they were dwelling on. Usually, they get the new dividing line which I made them draw between what they are responsible for and what they aren't (this is a manifestation of rule no. 18).

This is a very common mistake we make in our culture aside from the embeddedness it has in the language I am outlining here. The dividing line between what we are responsible for and what we aren't is blurred somewhere in our upbringing. This is the root of many problems within relationships, families, workplace situations, and just generally in our dealings with others. This is not exclusive to the Alcoholic/Addict family system. I tell people sitting in front of me all the time, 'You are only responsible for what you think, feel, and do'.

These concepts are not solution-oriented concepts. You can never rid yourself of them once accepted as a definition of yourself. They are all pervasively stuck on you. They are also myths. They don't exist unless we conjure them up in our own minds and nurture them through familial reinforcement. Clients have a hard time with this idea.

These concepts are part of the fencing that keeps everyone in the Alcoholic/Addict family system in the system. It's a way of maintaining emotional control of the members of the system. They all perceive this invisible barrier that they grew up with and maintain because it's what they know, it's what feels comfortable. We get used to the crunching of the eggshells we always feel we are walking on. Everything outside this system is unknown, and scarier than what we know. So, they follow the rules and stay in and maintain the system.

These concepts are locked into our culture from several different origins. They certainly have overtones much larger than just the Alcoholic/Addict methodology that I am outlining here. For my purpose, I define these as the fencing around this Alcoholic/Addict system that maintains the addiction and the system. I will draw on previous rules that I have given examples.

That kid in the classroom with circles under his eyes because he has been up all night and the teacher knows something is wrong. That child feels shame that these people, outsiders, will find out. The child is embarrassed by the chaos of the system at home. The child foreshadows guilt if a note or phone call comes home from school. He knows the reaction of the system to outside scrutiny. The child has no other frame of reference so maintain as best they can, what they know.

The wife (codependent) whose Alcoholic/Addict just impulsively got a puppy for the kids. She knows instinctively and from past experience, that the responsibility (rule no. 18) of the puppy will fall on her. She will buy into the excuse (rule no. 14) that the children need to learn responsibility is a good thing. She will still be the one that teaches whatever responsibility that the children glean from this experience. She will just incorporate this added responsibility to her already overburdened calendar of things to do that will maintain the system and keep her Alcoholic/Addict from having to suffer owning the responsibility of the situation.

Scapegoat or Identified Patient

17. We need a scapegoat (or identified patient)

This rule has to do more with the roles that we fall into in the Alcoholic/ Addict system. With children in the family, they will have a tendency to fall into certain roles. These will come about through birth order, sex of the children in the birth order, sex of the Alcoholic/Addict in the family, personality, or by default. They also depend on how many children or members of the family system are involved. These variables all play out in the Alcoholic/Addict family in unique ways that are similar to regular dysfunctional family systems but will exhibit their own independent peculiar natures.

The development and outcome for roles in the Alcoholic/Addict system are that the child or the children in the system, always observant and hypervigilant, understand that there are things that are not done by the adults. These are the things that are above the children's emotional pay grade, but one or a few of the children step up and get them done. They know they need to be done. They know they are not being done. After all, there is only so much responsibility (rule no. 18) that the codependent can take on from the Alcoholic/Addict. It is the children in the role of pleaser or, the fixer, or fixers, that pick up the slack in the Alcoholic/Addict family.

There is one more role that becomes very important in the Alcoholic/ Addict system. It is an insidious role that most times ruins the life of the role player. If they do not ever get counseling or have some insight as to their system function they may stay stuck in this role for life. This role plays out as the scapegoat of the family. It is also characterized as the Identified Patient in more clinical or academic circles. When independence of the system is finally gained without adequate insight or counseling intervention, they will fall into the role of lifelong victim. Everything will be against them. They feel or voice that they will never be able to accomplish anything. Their self-esteem will be elusive. Many times these members of the system grow up to be the Alcoholic/Addict themselves for their own family systems. In this way, the Language and Behavior get passed down through the generations.

I experienced a glaring example of this in the family of my now ex-wife. She came from a family of three. The birth order was female, female and male. They were all about one to two years apart. Her father was the Alcoholic/Addict and her mother was the codependent. It was a very traditional midwestern family setup. They were from Illinois.

Her father was a very strong-willed, male ego-driven man with old-school ideals. His genetics and socialization in the family came from a very Alcoholic/Addict Irish mother who had little emotional presence for her four children. He was the head of the house. What he said was the rule (rule no. 15). He was quite irreverent in his ways and speech which enamored his grandsons, my three boys. He was a large personality. someho

He treated his middle daughter as the scapegoat. She was the one in the family that always got blamed. If anything happened, anything went wrong she was on the hot seat for it. Everyone else in the family followed suit with this way of ditching responsibility (rule no. 18). There was always something in the family that was not quite on track. Something that was not acceptable to the Alcoholic/Addict in the family, in this system the father. She was the one that had to own the shame blame and guilt of whatever did not fit, look somehow imperfect or went wrong (rule no. 3) in the rigid family system.

An incident that was described to me that happened in the family was the shampoo. Their father had typical male pattern baldness. As many male ego-driven men of the 70's he did a comb-over so that one side of his hair was much longer than the other side. He had to use many hair products on it to get it to look like he had hair. I am sure the ritual of this was arduous. He went to use shampoo one day and it was nearly gone. His daughters used the expensive shampoo. His shampoo. He came downstairs with the bottle, met his middle daughter on the stairs, and banged her in the forehead with the bottle, knocking her backward down the stairs. He carried on yelling at her and blaming her for using up all his shampoo.

He focused on her as the bad actor, even though she was not the only one in the family that was using the shampoo. This was whether or not this was one of those unspoken rules set in the family or just another booby trap to initiate a blowup. She was always the one to get blamed. She had to be the focus of everything that went wrong in the family or that exemplified dysfunction from the family because he could not be responsible (rule no. 18) for anything. Everyone else followed suit with this line of reasoning because again, they also did not want to be responsible (rule no. 18).

This caused this second daughter to emulate her older sister, the one that looked good (rule no. 3), the one that was the fixer and pleaser (an extension of rule no. 17), the golden child of the family. There were some things and incidents that were related to me without the understanding of this context of their upbringing. This second daughter was born a year apart from the older sister. She got her period two weeks after her older sister. Her older sister got pregnant with her first child and it was announced through the family. The second daughter through a stormy on an off relationship which had been finished, several months after her sisters announcement was back together and pregnant with her first child. The desperate need for acceptance and to please and on some level compete with her sister was so strong that it even pushed her biological systems.

No Responsibility

18. We don't take responsibility

Responsibility is a hot potato in the Alcoholic/Addict family system. Some of this has to do with stress. Any added responsibility means more stress added to the system. Additional stress added to this system is intolerable because this system runs on very rigid lines. The Alcoholic/Addict will tend to act in impulsive ways that bring more responsibility and therefore stress to the system. This seems counterintuitive but it works to help maintain the behaviors in the system. The end result is the manufacture of random blowups in the system. This is a main feature of the system and creates many of the dysfunctional behaviors that manifest in the members of the system.

Responsibility takes many forms of aversion in an Alcoholic/Addict family. Expressed emotions are one of the ways responsibility gets avoided or offloaded onto others in the system, mainly the codependent or the fixers/ pleasers. Emotions are not well defined in the system (rule no. 6) or they get completely transferred to others because the added stress of these is intolerable.

The consequences of this learning process are all too predictable. We suppress our anger/emotion but don't understand that any suppressed emotion does not go away, it just morphs into something else and then rears up at times we don't want it to or are not prepared to experience it. "Irritability is anger that lacks self-knowledge."1 I have not found a quote that exemplifies this emotional process better than this. We suppress the appropriate feelings in this situation and they will find a way out. What happens is they find their way out in terms of blowups that start to occur in the relationships and families that we develop outside our Alcoholic/ Addict family of origin. And thus it is perpetuated.

First, the Alcoholic/Addict was raised in a similar environment with the same language and behaviors. This is their learned baseline from which they are to evolve. They grow up with limited coping skills (rule no. 11) and no emotional honesty (rule no. 6) to start out. Evolving from this baseline of socialization is difficult at best. Given how little we introspect in our culture, we tend to stay within the confines of this less effective way of communicating and behaving that our parents taught us. Within this, we don't learn to define the nuances of what we are responsible for and what we are not. We end up defaulting to what the system teaches; responsibility is a burden to be avoided and to be rid of.

Getting rid of responsibility is easier than it would seem when you are wellpracticed. The Alcoholic/Addict is full of promises.

"Yes, I will get the chores done by the time we leave."

"It will never happen again."

"Sure I will get the kids fed before you get home late"

"I will get to the lawn next Saturday."

"I thought I paid that bill already."

"Don't worry it will work itself out."

Of course, these don't get done or are not up to any set expectation, one more stressor. There are a million and one excuses (rule no. 14) for not taking on or ditching a responsibility. It was my memory, I had to do something else, I cannot keep up with all that YOU (rule no. 12) demand. These promises and the inevitable excuses for not following through are generally laid out in absolutes (rule no. 15). It is always or never. They do not have a middle-ground position. It is not in their repertoire.

Expectations

19. We have silent expectations

This rule is a late addition to the rules that I formulated for my approach to Addiction intervention. It is not unique to Alcoholic/Addict family systems. Like most dysfunctional ways of doing things in families, there need not be an addiction process to learn or lead an ineffective lifestyle in your family system of origin. I believe it needs inclusion here to emphasize the unique qualities that it brings to an addicted family process.

I have in my rules for conducting therapy in my private practice the idea that expectations sabotage therapy. They do. They also severely at times sabotage relationships we are in. When we have an idea that our spouse is going to behave in a certain way, we have already screwed up. We set an expectation, made an assumption, that they can never meet. The idea is in our head and most of the time we have not effectively communicated or out loud. No one can meet an expectation that they don't know about. Even when they understand and have heard what the desire coming from us is, it may be something so foreign to them that they won't or cannot accomplish it.

Couples that live together for years, that know each other as well as anyone, assume that they can anticipate their partner's thoughts, needs, and feelings. They cannot. They are only taking a guess based on past experience. The problems arise when the recipient of the assumption gets angry. "How dare you assume what I want." Their partner has once again missed the mark of what their needs are really. Alternately, the person trying to meet the unspoken assumed needs of their partner is upset when their efforts fall short in the other's reaction (another assumption). They might get irritable that they once again haven't lived up to assumed unspoken expectations.

This pattern of behavior is all too common and leads to frustration between partners and poor communication in the relationship. We think that we know the rules and that idea gets turned on its head when the first argument manifests then another and another. The analogy of this process I like to use with couples is Monopoly. We all know how to play Monopoly. We have been playing since we were kids. Then I ask, "Do you put $500 in the center for when you land on free parking?" "Do you put taxes in the center for when you land on free parking?" The funny thing is, we all know how to play Monopoly, but in the middle of the game, we realize that we understand very different rules. On top of this neither one of us has ever read the rules of Monopoly. We go into relationships this way, we all have a different set of rules that we have not decided on at the beginning.

How these assumptions and expectations translate to the Alcoholic/Addict family system is through the unspoken nature of how the rules are conveyed, learned, and carried out. There is already a system of unknown expectations in place that are the basis of the system. When these are not met, that is when the blowup (overreaction) takes place. These emotional explosions are the guidelines for the learning curve in the system. They are like guard rails that keep everyone doing the same thing in the same direction.

They help protect and isolate the system from the outside world.

Children growing up in this system learn not to touch these side rails very quickly through this intermittent punishment schedule1; random blowups. This learning process promotes the idea that if we behave a certain way we can control the outcome of others' behaviors. This is fallacious thinking taught to us through the circumstance of an Addicted Family system. "One's wants, needs, and desires end up being suppressed because they are not being talked about out loud. This of course works itself out along gender lines."2 This becomes a lifelong learned behavior that we mind in the system while under its yoke. It also becomes the way we conduct our relationships when we get out into the real world. Unfortunately, we meet similar souls from similar backgrounds and this dysfunctional way of doing things seems to work for a while. Soon enough the distorted dysfunctional nature of that lifestyle spins out without either party knowing what happened.

1. This reinforcement schedule is known to be the strongest and goes all the way back to Thorndike (1898). His study of Operant Conditioning showed how incredibly strong this intermittent reward/punishment learning process is. It is precisely the learning process that takes place in

Alcoholic/Addict families.

2. The School of Life, de Botton

Family Roles

As I have outlined previously, there are distinct roles that are molded by the Alcoholic/Addict family system. You have the Fixer, the Pleaser, the Good child (or Golden child), the Goat (or identified patient), the Rebel, and the Lost child (or addict). All these roles are learned and played out within the system based on experience, birth order, and individual resilience, and the amount of abuse that is meted out in the system and to whom.

The Fixer/Pleaser role are those children in the system that stepped up to the plate. There were things in the family household that were not getting done. They recognized that these things were not getting done and needed to get done. The parents, the Alcoholic/Addict and their Codependent, were busy with their symbiotic dysfunctional relationship and were not watching the farm. The Fixer/Pleaser child steps up and gets some things done around the house that needs to be done but are not getting done. This process can become a lifelong dysfunction. When we as children, try to keep the family system going by accomplishing the things that are not getting done, we know that we don't know how to do these things really. We do them anyway. That hypervigilant part of us is always looking over our shoulders to see if we are going to get yelled at for doing it wrong. Learning accomplishments this way never lets us derive self-esteem completely from the accomplishments. We never feel it's good enough or that we are good enough.

There is a dark side and a silver lining to this learning process.

The silver lining for children growing up in this system is that they turn out to be overachievers and pleasers. These are our Doctors, Nurses, Therapists, and Social Workers in the community that are still trying to fix things as they help. This is a silver lining to the process. It ends up benefiting society in a weird backward way.

The dark side of this learning process in molding these children in the Alcoholic/Addict family system is that they end up having feelings of what they call 'imposter syndrome'. In this role, we learn that things need to be done that aren't being done. We step up to the plate and get these things done. We are working way above our emotional pay grade in the family system. We know that we don't know how to do these things but do them anyway because they need to be done. Because we are already programmed to be hypervigilant of the next blowup, we do these things with the idea that at any moment someone will yell at us for doing it wrong. We are always on edge with what we are accomplishing. It becomes an ingrained way of accomplishing things so that we never really feel the sense of accomplishment we should. We don't learn to build our self-esteem well with what we do. This becomes a life long issue.

These people have trouble accepting compliments. They are the ones who shrink from accepting awards at work and self-deprecate when talking about what they have done. They attribute their accomplishments to others on their team. They never feel comfortable being solely responsible (rule no. 18) for what gets done. This is the essence of 'imposter syndrome' within the context of the Alcoholic/Addict family system.

The Good child tends to be the one that is a pleaser because they never step out of line, they don't draw attention to the family, and they always make sure they look good (rule no. 3). They are the face, the shining example of how wholesome the all-American family they came from is. Sadly they never get the emotional support that they need to have good self-esteem. They go out into the world and have less than satisfying relationships because they have not learned to develop those. They tend not to introspect so never really get to the bottom of their dysfunction. Others tend to look on them as shallow.

I outlined the role of the Goat or identified patient. This was my sister-inlaw. She was plugged into this role because the family needed someone to blame (rule no. 16) for the tension and dysfunction that was a constant in the family. These children don't ever feel they are getting the emotional support or attention they need. They will act out in ways to stand out and this is unacceptable to the Alcoholic/Addict system. They are going against the rules of calling negative attention to the family (rule no. 3). They end up getting in trouble and fulfilling the prophecy of being the problem child. They end up usually falling into an addiction and/or rarely really reaching their natural potential.

The Rebel is that child in the family that recognizes early on that things are dysfunctional. They have made the realization that there are much more functional ways of doing things. They may demand more emotional support and what they need from the family. The family of course is not capable of giving these things well or at all. The Rebel looks for ways to be more functional and is not afraid to entertain new ideas from the outside world. They get in trouble with the system because they also call attention to things not working and violate the rules (rule no. 3, and rule no. 4). These children are the ones that will entertain Therapy and work toward a more functional way of doing things.

The Lost child(ren) in the Alcoholic/Addict family system fall in the footsteps of their examples and become Alcoholic/Addicts themselves. They never really pay close attention to the family or what is happening. They are glad that their siblings are taking care of some of the things that aren't being taken care of but they are not ambitious enough to do anything about the deficits of the system. They are just keeping their head down. Their self-esteem suffers because they avoid what little attention is available in the family system because it is usually negative anyway. They have a tendency to be down the line in the sibling structure which makes them have a need to get things they want now and not wait. They have a need to feel good and discover substances that provide immediate gratification. They find an easy path to addiction and are the most susceptible to this coming out of the Alcoholic/Addict family system.

We live under this cloud of emotional suppression and role molding long enough that it becomes ingrained, second nature, all too familiar, and therefore comfortable as the status quo. This system teaches us to suppress our emotions and coupled with the self-esteem deficiency we derive from the system we learn that our emotions are not as important as others, or our partner. In most of these roles, we tend to subordinate ourselves in the relationships we find.

When things need to get done in our own lives, this system creates in us a

task paralysis where we become less than functional. We rationalize this (rule no. 14) by saying we are procrastinating. We learn this through either expectation of the criticism to come or that we already know that nothing is going to be good enough.

Addendum

I set out to develop a system of working with addiction in my private practice through my own ignorance of addiction and my apparent fundamental knowledge of the Alcoholic/Addict family system. It was my upbringing and journey of discovery of what I learned in this upbringing that brought me to put it into writing. Not all of these rules fit everyone that come from this Alcoholic/Addict family system. I believe it to be an approach that corrects some of the flaws of other interventions that I have observed.

First, an Addiction is an Addiction is an Addiction. We all do them the same way. Whether it is food, porn, gambling, cocaine, heroin, nicotine, sex, marijuana, caffeine, lifting weights, relationships, or any other substancc or cxtcrnal objcct or situation that is utilized to change a person's internal emotional state, we do them all the same way. We learn them the same way. We follow the same rules and behaviors of that learning that reinforces the addiction. If we continue the same behaviors and language even though we have sworn off whatever object was the problem, we relapse. It's not the Alcohol that makes you the Alcoholic, it is the language and behavior. This makes the language and the behavior the focus of any change that needs to take place for there to be a resolution to the addiction. This is my approach to resolving addiction in my clients.

www.ingramcontent.com/pod-product-compliance
Lightning Source LLC
Chambersburg PA
CBHW071358230926
51846CB00002B/590
* 9 7 8 1 9 7 0 4 6 3 3 7 8 *